D0724023

Never Give Up!

Short Stories about Big Dreams

Written by David Messick   Illustrated by Liu Light

Never Give Up!
Short Stories about Big Dreams
Written by David Messick
Illustrated by Liu Light

Never Give Up!
Short Stories about Big Dreams
© 2020 / All rights reserved

Text David Messick
Original Art Liu Light
Puppet Images Rainbow Productions, Inc.
Designed by Lynn Mangosing

ISBN: 978-1-7332484-3-3

Printed in the USA
Fourth Printing
Rainbow Puppet Publications
18 Easthill Court
Hampton, Virginia 23664

www.rainbowpuppets.com   info@rainbowpuppets.com

Rainbow Puppet Productions is a non-profit,
educational, entertainment company

*Special thanks to Curtis Johnson, Traci Massie, Erin Matteson,
David & Stephanie Messick, Marcy Messick, and Rose West*

Dedication

To my son, Luke Messick.
A beloved goal keeper, a great manager, and a
shining star!

And to my aunt, Beth Messick who once told me
"you should write a book about all those people
you talk about." Beth has the gift of
encouragement and hospitality.   Most of all, she
never gives up!

Contents

Introduction

When I was in elementary school my mother took me to see a touring New York theater production of "Young Tom Edison." What a great experience! In the darkened theater I saw Young Tom selling newspapers on a train and later causing an explosion when one of his experiments backfired. After many adventures, Tom Edison goes from a failure in school to an inventor celebrated the world over.

The story was inspiring. The play was magical. Then and there, I knew I wanted to create plays and stories and share them with others. My dad shared with me something I'll always remember. "You can do almost anything you set your mind to… as long as you're willing to work hard and never give up!"

What great advice. He was right. So we created Rainbow Puppets and started touring to schools, libraries, museums, and theaters. It took a lot longer than I dreamed it would and the journey was filled with disappointments, setbacks, and great happiness. Imagine performing in the Smithsonian… beside a Tuskegee airplane or the Wright Brothers' first flyer!

Here are some stories about people who had setbacks, disappointments, and yet they succeeded. What my dad said to me is just as true for you:

"You can do almost anything you set your mind to… as long as you're willing to work hard and never give up!"

Clockwise from top: David, Michael Singleton, James Cooper, and Tony Gabriele in front of the original Wright Brothers plane. *Rainbow Puppets*

Part 1:
Follow Your Dreams

Here's a group of folks
who had big dreams.
When the unexpected happened,
they found bigger dreams…

Walt Disney

Stolen Dreams

It's the spring of 1928 and Walt Disney is on a train headed from Hollywood to New York City. He's on top of the world. His company's new cartoon character "Oswald the Lucky Rabbit" has proven very lucky for Walt. The character is popular with the movie-going public and Walt now plans to renew his agreement to make more Oswald cartoons for more money. Unfortunately, Walt's luck is about to run out.

Walt Disney *NASA*

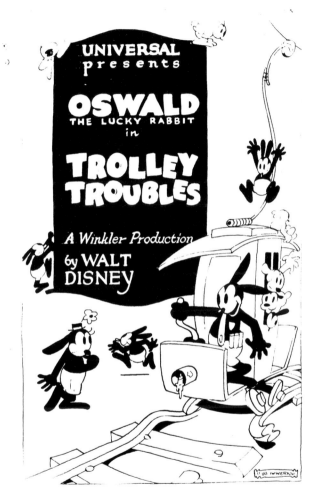

Original Poster for Oswald's first film. *Public domain*

When Walt arrives, he learns that his **distributor** has secretly made arrangements to take away most of Walt's artists and produce the cartoons himself. Instantly, Walt's dreams of a successful Hollywood career are all but destroyed.

So, does Walt give up?
No.

On the trip back to Hollywood he makes plans for a new character. When he gets back to his studio, he works with his brother Roy and his most talented animator, Ub Iwerks (pronounced "eye-works") to create a new character… a mouse. Walt comes up with story ideas as Ub races to draw and film the new character. They try selling it to other distributors but have no luck. Every studio has cartoons. They don't need any more.

Walt then develops a bigger plan. Until this point, movies were silent. They were presented with live musicians adding music in the background. But a new idea is being tried… adding voices and music to movies. The Warner Brothers movie studio has had a huge hit with a new "talking picture" called "The Jazz Singer."

But no one has tried adding sound to a cartoon… until now. Walt and Ub stop work on their silent cartoons and create an all-musical, all-talking cartoon. Drawings are created by Ub and story ideas are by Walt.

And there's more! Walt Disney provides the voice for their new character…

Mickey Mouse!

Mickey Mouse *Shutterstock*

The rest, as they say, is history. Mickey Mouse became an international sensation. And from this, Walt and his company went on to even greater success.

His company invented the feature-length cartoon with "Snow White," then pioneered television with "The Mickey Mouse Club," and then created the first of the company's many theme parks with the opening of Disneyland. As Walt would say, "I only hope that we don't lose sight of one thing — that it was all started by a mouse."

Walt and Mickey statue at Walt Disney World. *Depositphotos*

And the mouse
came about because
when Walt Disney
lost the rabbit…
he didn't give up!

P. T. Barnum

Dreams go up in smoke

The 2017 movie "The Greatest Showman" is one of the most **profitable** musicals of all time. P. T. Barnum, whose life inspired the movie, would be proud.

Billboard for "The Greatest Showman" *Faiz Zaki Shutterstock.com*

Barnum was a shipping clerk who dreamed of so much more. Drawn to the entertainment business, he was able to purchase a museum in New York City which he renamed "Barnum's American Museum."

P. T. Barnum with "General Tom Thumb"
Public domain

Through trial and error, he discovered what the public wanted and he gave it to them. He presented jugglers and magicians. He presented the amazing, like "General Tom Thumb," a performer who stood only three feet four inches tall.

He earned the title "King of Humbug" for attractions like "The Feejee Mermaid" which was actually a combination of a stuffed fish and monkey. Along the way, he also presented acts that were popular in their day but would be considered inappropriate by modern audiences.

To say his museum was popular would be an understatement. At times, Barnum's biggest problem was clearing the building to allow more visitors to enter.

Barnum's Mermaid was scary looking… nothing like this.
Rainbow Puppets

Here again he used his clever showmanship. He put up signs throughout the museum: "This way to the **egress**!" People would follow the signs through the building. They'd end up going through the door labeled "Egress" only to find themselves outside the museum. "Egress" was another word for "Exit!" People would then have to pay if they wanted to enter again.

Barnum's fame continued to grow until his museum business was destroyed by two horrible fires.

Barnum's American Museum on fire.
Everett Collection Shutterstock.com

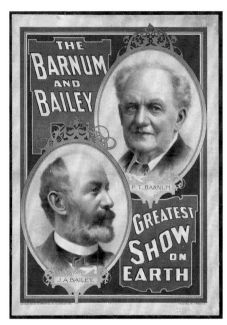

Instead of creating yet another building that people would come to visit, Barnum came up with a new dream. He'd take his show on the road. He'd take his amazing museum across the country.

Original posters. *Public Domain*

And so began "P. T. Barnum's Greatest Show on Earth." By partnering with other successful showmen, he began a touring entertainment business that ran for 147 years!

And it all happened because
when disaster struck,
P. T. Barnum didn't give up.

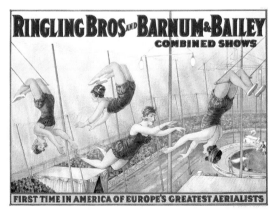

Original posters. *Public Domain*

Elvin Bale

⭐

Never give up.

In the darkened arena, the ringmaster announces, "Ladies and gentlemen, children of all ages, please direct your attention to the center ring. Here to defy gravity and tempt danger, we proudly present the greatest daredevil in circus history.

The one… the only… Elvin Bale."

Spotlights pick out a blond man who drops his cape and reaches for a rope that leads to the top of the arena. Elvin Bale then extends his legs forward and climbs up to the ceiling using only his arm strength. He makes his way onto a trapeze and begins to swing back and forth over the audience.

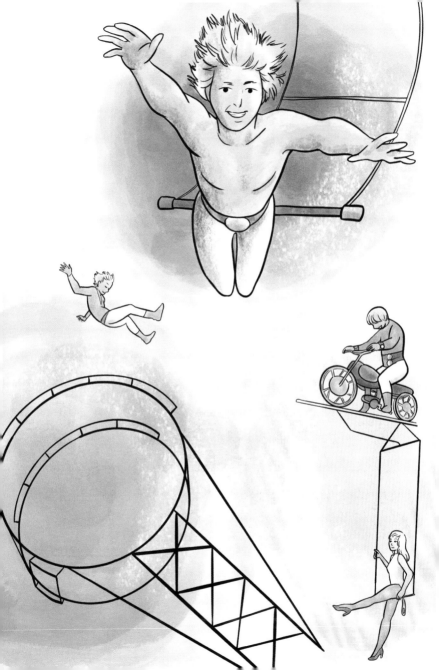

As he swings fully forward, and without the benefit of a net, he leaps off the trapeze to almost certain death. Members of the audience scream but there's no need to fear. At the last minute, Elvin catches himself with only his heels!

"The World's Largest Cannon" *Author*

Later in the show, he drives a motorcycle along a steel cable that runs high above the audience's head. His beautiful assistant sits below the

Promotional photo of Elvin Bale *Cassandra Bale Ingle*

motorcycle on a trapeze. He then follows up racing blind-folded across a huge steel contraption called "The Wheel of Death." The show ends with Elvin being shot across the entire length of the arena from "The World's Largest Cannon." He safely lands in an inflatable cushion as the audience erupts in cheers.

Elvin's courage and style earned him the greatest award in circus performing, the Gold Clown. He displayed his skills for Pope John Paul II as the only circus star to perform inside the Vatican.

Success followed success until January 8, 1987. A mistake was made setting up the cannon while performing in Hong Kong. The countdown went as planned. Elvin shot out of the cannon as usual but he sailed past the safety cushion. Elvin landed, breaking his ankles, his legs, and his spine.

He was told that his circus career was over. He was told that he would never walk again.

But this was Elvin Bale. He was determined to prove himself. A year later, he was standing and walking through the use of specially designed crutches. The amazing arm strength he used in his act now allowed him to walk again.

As for his circus career, Elvin knew more about presenting an act with flair and excitement than almost anyone on the planet. He now shared those skills with others.

Elvin Bale on the lot of the Cole Brothers Circus
Marcy Messick

He taught others to safely present the cannon act and other circus feats. From there, Elvin became the Vice President and Performance Director for the Cole Brothers Circus, "the world's largest circus under the big top!"

Dick Van Dyke introduces Elvin on a TV special *Cassandra Bale Ingle*

Elvin helped future stars follow their dreams in the circus. To Elvin's many fans, he became an even bigger star because he didn't give up.

Part 2:
Success out of Failure

*It feels great to succeed and
not so great to fail. Believe it or not,
two of the world's greatest inventions
came about because of repeated failures
that led to amazing success.*

Thomas Edison

Let There Be Light

Going back to the beginning of time, when the sun went down the world could become a scary place filled with dread and monsters, real and imagined. The use of candles, the invention of the safety match, and oil lighting all helped bring light into the dark of night. But it would take a persistent inventor and **innovator** named Thomas Edison to **revolutionize** lighting.

Young Thomas Edison's school teachers had no faith in his ability to learn or accomplish anything. They sent him home with a note to his mother saying he was unteachable. Fortunately, Tom's mother didn't share his teachers' beliefs and she didn't share the

note with him. Instead, she taught him at home, making sure he read on a wide variety of subjects.

And Tom excelled. His first major invention was a talking machine that could reproduce voices and music on a spinning cylinder.

Now Thomas Edison had a bigger vision. What if there was a safer way to bring light to everyone? To be clear, Edison did NOT invent the first light bulb. The idea of allowing electricity across a thin wire or thread **filament**, all encased in a sealed glass bulb, was studied and created by others.

Edison believed the basic idea was correct but more work was needed on the filament inside the glass bulb. The filament materials were either too costly or didn't burn long enough to be practical.

And so, he and his scientists tested… and failed.

And tested… and failed… and tested… and failed.
Over and over again.

In all, they tried over 6,000 different plant materials
trying to find the right one. Some would light up for a
while but quickly burn out. Others never lit up at all.

In Edison's mind, these experiments were not failures at all, saying...

"I have not failed. I've just found 10,000 ways that won't work."

Edison would just keep trying until he got it right. He knew it would take hard work to succeed. As he famously said, "Genius is one percent inspiration, ninety nine percent perspiration."

In the end, Edison and his company did find a successful way to manufacture bulbs that would light up the world. They used **carbonized** cotton thread as the filament which glowed fourteen hours. This was later improved with a carbonized bamboo filament which lasted much longer. He would go on to innovate motion pictures and come up with over one thousand other **patented** ideas.

Thomas Edison. *Public domain*

*And it all happened because
Edison believed in his hunches...
and he never gave up.*

The Wright
Brothers

and the Wrong Formula

The wind gust blew sand along the dunes of Kitty Hawk, North Carolina on that cold December 17th, 1903. No one would believe what happened if not for a picture snapped by John T. Daniel. That picture became one of the most famous taken in the last century.

Statue of John T. Daniel.
Depositphotos

The First Flight. *Public Domain*

For 12 seconds, with his brother Wilbur watching, Orville Wright flew the first self-powered airplane in history.

Inventors with government help around the world were racing to be the first. No one expected that the honor would go to two bicycle builders from Dayton, Ohio.

The Wright Brothers had no formal training beyond high school. But they did have a secret weapon… they came from a supportive family that valued reading and study. Unlike most households of the day, there were two libraries full of books in their home. One for general reading and one to support their father's work as a traveling minister.

Even at a young age, they knew that almost anything they wanted to learn could be found inside the pages of a book.

As young men, they became part of the bicycle craze that swept the country. For a modest amount of money, people could travel long distances on their own. They opened a bicycle shop but soon turned their attention toward dreams of flight.

Orville and Wilbur devoured every book they could find. They then wrote to scientists around the world

who frequently would answer their questions. They reached out to the Smithsonian Institution in Washington, D.C., asking for more information. Again, they were favored with more materials.

Through analysis and study, they determined that they needed to solve three issues:

POWER,
to move the machine forward

LIFT,
to rise up off of the ground

CONTROL,
to steer out of danger

To solve the issue of power, the brothers determined that most motors available would be too heavy.

Wesley Huff, Alyssa Jones, Joshua Messick in performance with Orville and Wilbur Wright. *Rainbow Puppets*

They needed to craft an engine with just enough power to lift one person and their craft in the air. They received help from a friend to build just such a motor.

To solve the issue of lift, they would build their glider wings following the formulas that other inventors had already developed.

To solve the issue of control, they created a unique system where they could lie on the glider and shift their hips to steer the glider to the left or the right.

Armed with their knowledge, they traveled to the soft, sandy beaches of North Carolina to test their ideas.

Pixabay

The brothers would take turns lying down on their kite-like gliders and try to soar into the sky. Sometimes they would float a bit, but never as well as they hoped. And sometimes they failed. Sometimes, quite painfully. After one notable crash,

Wilbur picked himself up off of the ground and reportedly said, "Not within a thousand years will man ever fly!"

They had followed the formulas exactly and kept crashing to the ground. Wilbur said, "I'm going back home to Dayton to build bicycles."

As brothers, they had the ability to encourage each other when one would lose faith. Orville replied,

"We're going back home to Dayton, but not to give up."

"We have followed the formulas exactly and we have failed. I don't believe it's us. I believe there's something wrong with the formulas. We're going back home and we're going to find out the right formula!"

Testing inside a modern wind tunnel. *NASA*

And that's just what they did. They created a wind tunnel and other instruments to test and determine the correct formula.

Years later, NASA scientists, using sophisticated computers and wind tunnels confirmed what the world would soon learn…

For the 100th Anniversary of flight, Rainbow Puppets performed near the Wright Memorial, just yards from the spot of the first flight. *Rainbow Puppets*

The Wright Formula was the right formula for flight!

The Brothers made it into the history books. They are celebrated with monuments and museums in North Carolina and Ohio. Their original flyer is now found at the National Aviation and Space Museum in Washington, DC..

Pixabay

And all because the Wright Brothers never gave up!

Part 3:
Be Persistent

Hockey great Wayne Gretzky once said, "You miss 100% of the shots you don't take." Here is a group of folks who stayed in the game. They kept at it when others thought they were finished. They kept at it when others wouldn't let them on the team. They kept at it even when they weren't feeling their best. And they all succeeded!

Mickey Rooney

The Best Days Are Coming!

By the late 1970's many show business experts were saying Mickey Rooney's best days were behind him. Sure, he was the star of his own silent movie series when he was a child. But that was 50 years ago… and no one was making silent movies anymore. Sure, he was the biggest movie star

Mickey and Judy Garland on the radio.
Courtesy Everett Collection - stock. adobe.com

in the entire world back when he was making movie musicals with Judy Garland at MGM movie studios.

But those big musicals were a thing of the past, and MGM was selling off its costumes, sets, and backlot. Between each of Mickey's great successes, he had periods of failure, unemployment, and disappointment. But Mickey chose not to live in the past. Instead, he would give a wink, flash his fabulous smile, and say, "You always pass failure on the way to success."

And his next success was on the way. Broadway **producer** Harry Rigby had a vision of Mickey starring on Broadway in a musical filled with old jokes and songs. He'd team Mickey up with tap-dancing sensation Ann Miller in a show called "Sugar Babies."

The show became the talk of Broadway where they presented 1,208 performances. The show played for nine years with tours in America and England.

He followed this by winning an Emmy ® Award, two Golden Globe Awards, an honorary ACADEMY AWARD,® and a fourth star on the Hollywood Walk of Fame which he shared with his wife, Jan. He even provided voices for Walt Disney's "The Fox and the Hound"

Mickey and Jan Rooney *Depositphotos*

and for seven of Rainbow Puppet shows, including "A Pirate Party" and "Toyland!"

"A Pirate Party" *Rainbow Puppets*

Mickey spent over 90 years as a performer… and the awards kept coming, because he didn't give up!

Two Legends

with Great Advice

Michael Jordan

The NBA website says "Michael Jordan is the greatest basketball player of all time."

Pretty impressive statement about someone who didn't make his high school varsity basketball team during his sophomore year.

With all of his fame and impressive skill he reminds us, "I've missed more than 9,000 shots in my career. I've lost almost 300 games. 26 times I've been trusted to take the game-winning shot and missed.

Michael Jordan *Depositphotos*

*I've failed over and over and over
again in my life. And that is
why I succeed."*

Michael Jordan's comments are echoed by another legend from another sport.

Wilma Rudolf

Wilma Rudolph was given the title "fastest woman in the world." But she didn't start out that way. As a child, she contracted the polio virus. As she told it, "I walked with braces until I was at least nine years old. My life wasn't like the average person who grew up and decided to enter the world of sports."

Fortunately for Wilma, she had a mother who encouraged and believed in her. "My doctors told me I would never walk again. My mother told me I would. I believed my mother."

Through hard work, she got rid of the braces, became a runner and represented the USA at the Summer Olympics in Rome.

She ended up with three Gold Medals in track and field.

Wilma Rudolph winning the 100-meter dash at the 1960 Summer Olympics in Rome. *Giuseppina Leone*

Wilma didn't give up, and she offers some great advice: "Never underestimate the power of dreams."

Carol Channing

Don't Miss Your Best Performance!

If there was ever a performer who would not miss a chance to do her job, it was Carol Channing. You may have heard her one-of-a-kind raspy voice as Ms. Fieldmouse in the movie "Thumbelina" or as the glamorous octopus in Rainbow Puppet's "Pirate Party."

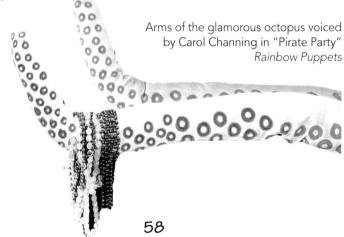

Arms of the glamorous octopus voiced by Carol Channing in "Pirate Party"
Rainbow Puppets

Carol Channing with President Lyndon B. Johnson after performing at the White House.*Courtesy Everett Collection - stock.adobe.com*

But long before those roles, she was a huge Broadway star. She introduced the song "Diamonds are a Girl's Best Friend," then went on to become a legend in the musical "Hello, Dolly!"

Carol appeared as the character Dolly Levi 5,000 times! She performed the role on Broadway, on tours around the country, and even brought the

Carol Channing's dance with LL Cool J inspired the song and character she portrayed in "Pirate Party." *Reuters Photographer - stock.adobe.com*

show right into then President Lyndon Johnson's White House. She was proud to say she never missed a performance.

Through sore throats, broken bones, and even through cancer treatments, she never missed a show.

She would share advice to others about how important it was to work through challenges and find new ways to do your job when you aren't feeling great. She felt that you would find new ways to communicate and work. "If you call off when you're not feeling great, you may deprive yourself of giving one of the best performances of your life."

Carol Channing performed and brought joy to many… because she didn't give up!

Part 4:
Let Your Voice
Be Heard

It's great to be heard. It's great to be recognized. But what if people laugh every time you open your mouth? With the next three stories, you'll meet people who overcame their difficulties and found success.

James Earl Jones

An Unlikely Legend

Darth Vader from "Star Wars" *Stefano Buttafoco Shutterstock.com*

It's a shocking scene that will be remembered
forever in movie history. Luke Skywalker is fighting

for the forces of goodness in a battle with the evil Darth Vader. Their light sabers flash and spark with each crashing blow. As Luke clings with one arm to a railing, he blames Darth Vader for killing his father. Darth Vader moves in closer and replies… "No, Luke. I am your father!"

It would be hard to pick a more memorable and thrilling voice than Darth Vader. And that voice was provided by the gifted actor, James Earl Jones.

If you had asked a young James Earl Jones if he could have imagined making a career with his voice, he would have been more shocked than Luke in that classic scene. You see, James Earl Jones stuttered in school. He could think of the words he wanted to say, but they didn't come out properly. Instead, he would repeat syllables without control. His classmates would laugh.

Fortunately for James Earl Jones, a force for good entered his life in the form of Donald Crouch, a teacher who recognized that James had a warm

voice and a gift for writing poetry. He encouraged him to practice speaking by reading his poetry in class. He had faith in James and worked with him until his stutter disappeared.

James Earl Jones *Everett Collection Shutterstock.com*

Through Donald's gifts as a teacher, the voice that caused shame and embarrassment transformed into one of the great voices on stage, television, and film.

Fortunately for film-goers, James Earl Jones didn't give up!

Geoffrey Holder

I Found My Voice!

Geoffrey Holder. *Rainbow Puppets*

The Waxy Monkey Tree Frog is a tiny creature that lives in South America. While he is small in size, he is noted for his loud and impressive voice. When Rainbow Puppets was searching for the perfect voice for this creature, to narrate "Amazon Adventures," only one actor came to mind… Geoffrey Holder.

Born in the island nation of Trinidad and Tobago, his wonderful laugh and booming voice, coupled with his huge size, helped him create memorable impressions as Punjab in the movie "Annie" and as a brilliant spokesperson on television.

In the studio, Mr. Holder shared that he grew up having great difficulty reading and speaking. A disability called **dyslexia** caused written words to jumble in his mind. It also made it difficult for him to find the right words to say, even when he was not reading. As a result, students would laugh at him whenever it was his turn to speak. As painful as this was for Geoffrey, he came to believe that this condition helped him discover new ways to communicate.

Geoffrey developed a talent for painting, dancing, and designing. Those skills brought him to the attention of the art world elite in New York City where Geoffrey thrived. At a meeting of other artists, he overheard people speaking of his former home in Trinidad… and their comments were not

Geoffrey and his wife, dancer Carmen de Lavallade
Carl Van Vechten

right. Geoffrey couldn't hold his opinions any longer and spoke up. Almost, magically, as all eyes in the room turned to him, he found the courage and the ability to correctly put his words and ideas together. He shared the joy and beauty of his homeland. At that moment, he found his voice.

Geoffrey went on to great heights in many different artistic arenas. He became a memorable character in a James Bond movie. His direction and design work for the "The Wiz" on Broadway earned him two Tony Awards. ®

He even provided the voice of a very loud and memorable Tree Frog, because when Geoffrey Holder faced difficulties, he didn't give up!

(Drums beat and horns begin to blare as the stage shakes... a large fan of leaves rises up center. The fan rises higher and higher and shakes more and more as the music builds to a crescendo... The leaves fall with an explosive sound to reveal...a tiny Tree Frog. He is small, almost neon yellow-green, and is dwarfed by the lily pad that he floats upon.)

(With an explosive laugh) Ha, Ha, Ha, Ha. Welcome to the Amazon! Ha, Ha, Ha, Ha!

You look disappointed. What? Were you expecting a T-Rex? He got lost along the way. But my ancestors survived!

Were you expecting a Mastodon? He got long in the tooth! Ha, Ha, Ha, Ha! But again my ancestors survived!

Yes. We survived. And we've seen it all... here in the Amazon.

Yes, here in the Amazon, things aren't as th___ me to introduce myself. I am Mon-tee, th___ Tree Frog. And to set the record straight, ___ Tax... I am not a tree... and I am definitely ___ ut I am a frog.

Geoffrey Holder created the
very big voice for the very small Waxy
Monkey Tree Frog in Rainbow's "Amazon Adventures."
Here is his marked script and the puppet. *Rainbow Puppets*

71

Tim Howard's

Random Acts

Tim Howard. *AGIF Shutterstock.com*

Soccer great Tim Howard is one of the sport's most
celebrated goal keepers. He has now added sports
commentator to his list of accomplishments.

It's unlikely that Tim would have ever dreamed of such a job. When he was 13, he was diagnosed with **Tourette Syndrome**. It's a disorder which

Tim Howard. *Alicia Chelini Shutterstock.com*

can cause unwanted tics like coughing, sniffing, and face movements. For Tim, it also led to him loudly clearing his throat at **inappropriate** times and caused an uncontrollable urge to touch items a specific number of times, over and over, for no apparent reason.

Tim found a way to control these symptoms and actually believes that the syndrome gave him the ability to intensely focus on the game.

Though he struggled through his early years, he didn't give up and is now a legend and role model on and off of the field

Part 5:
Don't Take "No"
for an Answer

Sometimes a "no" will keep you safe.
"No! Don't play with matches!"
"No! Don't go into those shark-infested
waters." At other times, "no"
may be a way of getting closer
to a "yes" and fulfilling your dreams.
Here are a group of folks who
heard "no." Some of them heard "no"
many times… and yet, they found
their way to "yes!"

Sandra Day O'Connor

No Girls Allowed!

Sandra Day was born on a ranch in Texas. As a little girl, she had no electricity or plumbing in her home. But she did have the chance to ride a horse, rope a cow, shoot a gun, drive the truck to get around the huge open spaces, and even change the tires.

She excelled in school and at age 16, she was accepted to Stanford University where she graduated with honors and went on to get her law degree.

After school, she couldn't get a job as a lawyer.

She was told time and again that women couldn't be lawyers. The best she was offered was a job as a secretary, working for other lawyers.

For someone who could rope a cow, shoot a gun, or change a tire, she would have none of that. Instead, she proposed that she would work as a

President Ronald Reagan and newly appointed Supreme Court Justice Sandra Day O'Connor. *White House Photo*

Sandra Day O'Connor opened the door for other female Supreme Court Justices including Sonia Sotomayor, Ruth Bader Ginsburg, and Elena Kagan. *Steve Petteway, Photographer for The Supreme Court of the United States*

President Obama gives Justice O'Connor the Presidential Medal of Freedom
REUTERS/Jason Reed
stock.adobe.com

deputy county attorney for no money to prove a woman could do the work. She did prove her abilities through hard work and excellent negotiating skills. She was appointed to fill a vacant Arizona Senate seat, received several court appointments, and eventually was nominated by President Ronald Reagan to became the first woman on the US Supreme Court, the highest court in the land.

Sandra would share that "There is no substitute for hard work." She created opportunities for herself and others because she wouldn't take "no" for an answer.

José Hernandez

11 Times No!

José Hernandez was born in California and spent his early years traveling from town to town helping his family harvest crops. As a migrant worker, he moved from one school to another and didn't learn to speak English until

José Hernandez in uniform. *NASA image*

he was 12 years old. He was, however, an excellent student and became an electrical engineer.

But José had bigger dreams. He wanted to be an astronaut. He worked hard and applied for astronaut training, but was told "no." He tried again, and was told "no." In fact, he was told "no" and turned down eleven times. But on the twelfth time, he was accepted.

Josef Schmid and José Hernandez *NASA*

José went on to become an aquanaut, doing research underwater, and finally, an astronaut on the space shuttle.

He accomplished this, and so much more, because he didn't take "no" for an answer and he didn't give up!

J. K. Rowling

12 Times No!

Imagine being the company that told J. K. Rowling, "No! We don't want to publish your book." The Harry Potter book series has sold over 500 million copies. It created generations of new readers. It

created blockbuster films. The Harry Potter Wizarding World has been recreated at

J.K. at a book event. *S. Bukley Shutterstock.com*

theme parks. And that's not to mention all the dolls, toys, games, wands, and costumes.

J. K. Rowling was a struggling mother, who came up with the idea of the fantasy world of Harry and his friends. She wrote the book as she could find time. But it was rejected by one publisher after another. It was rejected twelve times in all.

Fortunately for readers, movie goers, and theme park lovers around the world, J. K. Rowling didn't take

Hogwarts Castle at Universal Studios in Japan.
Adobe Stock

"no" for an answer and her book was published.

J. K. Rowling didn't give up!

Harland Sanders

1,009 Times No!

It would be
hard to miss
the face of the
kindly gentleman
smiling from a
sign on a KFC
restaurant.

Shutterstock

After all, KFC is one of the largest restaurant
chains in the world. Perhaps you've even seen the
character Colonel Sanders portrayed by one of many
actors on television.

In real life, the "Colonel" was Harland Sanders who

The real "Colonel" Sanders, signing an autograph for a young fan.
Edgy01 at English Wikipedia

started the restaurant and invented their original fried chicken recipe many years ago. At the age of 65, when most people his age were thinking of retiring, Harland Sanders found himself at the end of a long string of bad luck and business failures.

All he had to show for his years of work was a small Social Security check and a secret recipe and technique for creating what he thought was the best fried chicken in the world.

In days before fast food restaurants were found at practically every major street corner, Harland thought he could convince local stores to offer his fried chicken. He thought that once they tasted his chicken, they couldn't say no.

Shutterstock

So, Harland packed up his pressure cooker along with his secret recipe and started driving around the country. He'd fry up the chicken and try to sell his idea to anyone with a store. He traveled the country, often sleeping in his car. But the answer was always the same… "no!"

And we're not talking about one "no" or even two. He heard "no" 1,009 times! But he didn't give up. He didn't stop. At his 1,010th stop he found someone who understood his vision and loved his chicken.

That one "yes" turned into thousands of **franchised** stores that can now be found around the world.

At an age when many people would think of ending their career, "Colonel" Sanders became a millionaire because he didn't give up.

Part 6:
It CAN Be Done!

Just because someone else
says "it can't be done"
doesn't make it true.
Here's a group of people
who did what "couldn't be done."
Along the way, they managed
to open doors and help others.

George Washington Carver

⭐

You Can't Do Anything with Sweet Potatoes!

George Washington Carver was a gifted man. He was able to combine his education as a scientist with his belief in God to help his fellow, newly-freed slaves find success and independence.

Carver believed that all plants and all creatures could coexist successfully only when they worked together in good balance. His insight helped a nation of farmers.

After the Civil War, freed slaves and other poor

George Washington Carver *Public Domain*

southerners had no land and no job. Many became sharecroppers. They would plant on land owned by someone else in exchange for some of the profits from their work. If they had a good planting year, they might make a small profit. If they had a bad year, they would have to borrow money from the land owner to buy food and supplies to get through the winter. Carver saw that many of his countrymen were getting deeper and deeper in debt to land owners with no hope of real freedom.

One of the problems was cotton. Buyers wanted cotton to make fabrics. It was considered a "cash crop." The trouble with growing cotton was that the plants took a lot of nutrients from the soil. Without expensive fertilizers, which the sharecroppers could not afford, the land eventually became dry and useless.

That's where Carver's gifts came to the rescue. He discovered that some plants, like peanuts and sweet potatoes, actually added nutrients back into the soil. By switching from cotton to peanuts and sweet potatoes in **rotation**, the land would find balance and reward the farmers.

But the farmers were skeptical. "It can't be done." Nobody wants to buy peanuts and sweet potatoes. What are they good for?

Photo of Peanuts *Spice Teller at Pixabay*

Carver went to his laboratory to see what he could make from peanuts and sweet potatoes. Legend would tell you that he invented peanut butter. The truth is that **patent** belongs to John Harvey Kellogg of Kellogg's cereal fame. But Carver created so many more uses.

First, as a food, peanuts are rich in protein which made it a good part of the diet for poor farmers who could not afford meat. Beyond that, he created almost 300 other uses including shaving cream, flour, wood stains, skin lotion, paper, wall board, chili sauce, instant coffee, vinegar, milk, soap, dyes, paints, fuel, oils, ink, and lots of delicious peanut treats.

Then there were his ideas for the sweet potato. It's been called one of nature's perfect foods because it can be stored for long periods of time and it is very nutritious. Carver found ways to make sweet potatoes into paints, medicine, ink, artificial silk and cotton, molasses (a sweet syrup for cooking), doughnuts, flour, sugar, and 14 different kinds of candy.

Photo of Sweet Potatoes *Pixabay*

Carver took his ideas on the road and educated poor farmers across the country on how to find success and independence. Through his gifts, many were able to find the joy of success, saved money, purchased their own land, and found the pride of independence.

They were able to benefit from George Washington Carver's amazing gifts because George Washington Carver didn't give up on finding new ways to grow and use plants.

Bessie Coleman

Girls Can't Fly!

Bessie Coleman's family were sharecroppers in Texas. Her father was a Native American and her mother was African American. Her community had a one room school house four miles from her home where she could learn. Every year at harvest time, she'd have to leave her studies to help her family pick cotton under the burning sun.

Bessie Coleman *Public Domain*

Bessie would often look up at the birds flying overhead and dream that she could be free to fly wherever she wanted in the world.

Through hard study and savings, she was able to attend college for one year. Bessie's money ran out and she eventually ended up in Chicago with her brothers. While working at the White Sox Barber Shop, she heard amazing stories of World War I pilots. She wanted to fly. She knew she could do it.

As Bessie shared her dream, she heard many reasons why it couldn't happen. "Nobody's gonna let a woman fly! And they sure aren't gonna let a black woman fly!" "The only place they let any woman fly is France! And you aren't in France and you can't speak French!"

A local publisher heard about Bessie's dream and told the community to help out. Bessie learned how to speak French, and with the help of others, found her way to Paris, France.

In 1921, she became the first Native American and the first black woman with a pilot's license. She returned to America and created a sensation.

This was the time of daredevil pilots who would thrill the public with amazing air show tricks.

Bessie became known for her loop-de-loop and figure-eight tricks in the sky.

As she became more famous, she used her fame to make a difference for others. Some fairgrounds where she was to perform would not allow black citizens to attend, others would make black citizens enter through a different gate than white attendees. When Bessie heard, she would refuse to perform until everyone was allowed to enter through the same front gate.

Bessie's dreams of flight helped open doors to others and her dreams came true because she worked hard and never gave up.

Smithsonian Institute National Air and Space Museum educator Diane Kidd as Bessie Coleman with a member of the Pennsylvania Air National Guard and Astronaut Alvin Drew. *NASM*

"Chief" Charles Anderson

Tuskegee Men Can't Fly!

C. ALFRED "CHIEF" ANDERSON
Aviator
USA
70
2014

"Chief" Anderson was honored on a postage stamp.

While Bessie Coleman's dream of flight came true, she didn't live long enough to realize another dream. She always wanted to create a flight school to help others learn to fly. That dream was realized by someone else.

Charles Alfred Anderson had dreams of flight but he could find no one willing to teach a black man to fly. Undeterred, he bought an airplane. By observation, trial and error, and luck, Anderson taught himself to fly. In fact, he became a gifted pilot with the ability to take off and land with ease.

Anderson was not content to merely learn how to fly. Once he realized his goal, he wanted to share with others. He found himself at the Moton Field at the Tuskegee Institute in Alabama.

Black men from around the country came to learn from Anderson… "Chief" Anderson

Moton Field is a National Historical Site. The U.S. Mint is commemorating the site on a coin. *US Mint*

as they now called him. The Chief took time not only to teach flying, he knew each of his students personally. He knew their family stories, their struggles in school, and more. He was a **mentor**.

As World War II approached, the pilots in Alabama wanted to serve their country as airmen. At the time, no one in the military would let them fly. Rumors were spread that no one in Tuskegee *could* fly.

Somehow, those rumors made their way to Washington, D.C., where Eleanor Roosevelt, the president's wife heard. Eleanor was a kind-hearted but very shrewd woman. She knew a way to help the men in Tuskegee. She would go down to Alabama herself and she was sure the photographers of the press would follow.

"I've been told you have an airfield. I've even been

The famous picture of Eleanor Roosevelt flying with Charles Anderson
US Navy

told you have pilots and yet I don't see a single
plane in the sky!" she said on arrival.

Soon, Charles Anderson's team of fliers filled
the sky with airplanes. And to add to the sight,
Mrs. Roosevelt got into a plane with Chief Anderson.
"Now, wait for the pictures, Mr. Anderson.

That's very important!" said Mrs. Roosevelt as they smiled for the cameras.

The news was out. The proof was there. Those men in Tuskegee, Alabama could fly.

Ezra Hill, Sr. and other Tuskegee Airmen received a gold medal at the White House. He later narrated shows for Rainbow Puppets.
White House Photograph

Ezra Hill, Tuskegee Airman, puppet used in shows by Rainbow Puppets
Rainbow Puppets

Soon, they were accepted into the service and worked on legendary bombing missions to fight the evil Nazis who were trying to take over the world.

The Tuskegee Airmen became celebrated heroes, recognized by their peers and by Presidents.

They became legends because of a clever First Lady and a flying instructor who never gave up!

Meinhardt Raabe

Over the Rainbow…
into the Clouds!

It's 1941 and the United States has been drawn into the Second World War with both Japan and Germany. After the bombing of our naval base in Hawaii, Americans were now anxious to defend their country. Men raced to recruiting stations to enlist in the Army, Navy, and Marines.

While his friends and neighbors were being accepted, one man only heard "No! You're too short!" That man was Meinhardt Raabe (pronounced Mine-heart Robby). At three feet six inches high,

Meinhardt was short, and proud of it. He also was not used to giving up.

Earlier in his life, when Meinhardt heard there was a world's fair coming and they wanted small people to work a miniature circus, he immediately got a job. Because of his excellent speaking and selling skills, he became their "barker." That's the person who stands by the entrance of attractions to build up an audience.

When Meinhardt heard that the Oscar Mayer meat company was looking for a traveling sales person, he became the first "Little Oscar," traveling across the territory in their newly-created "Wienermobile."

When Meinhardt heard that Hollywood was looking to hire as many "little people" as they could for a new movie called "The Wizard of Oz," he headed off to California. He not only was hired, but was given

Original lobby card for "The Wizard of Oz." That's Meinhardt on the left of Dorothy, holding the certificate. *Public Domain*

the role of "Coroner Munchkin." He was the official in the purple costume who said the evil Witch of the East was "really, most sincerely dead."

Born in Watertown, Wisconsin, he was influenced by the character of his Lutheran, German farmer family. If you want to eat, you work. You don't waste time or opportunities. If you want it, go for it. Meinhardt's family made no exceptions for his short height. That thinking served Meinhardt well. As World War II called for all Americans to help out... Meinhardt insisted that he would be a good citizen and do his part.

Meinhardt soon learned that pilots who passed the age and height requirements had been recruited to serve overseas. But that left America vulnerable to attacks from Japanese and German soldiers. More pilots were needed at home. Meinhardt used his sales talents to convince a local pilot to teach him to fly, and Meinhardt soon got his pilot's license.

(Opposite page) Two worlds collide in this picture. Meinhardt is standing on the Wienermobile portraying Oscar Mayer's "Little Oscar." In the background, the theater is showing "The Wizard of Oz." *Watertown Historic Society*

Meinhardt provided the voice of a small but fierce piranha in Rainbow Puppet's "Amazon Adventures." *Rainbow Puppets*

He was admitted into the Civil Air Patrol. Because of his height, there was no official uniform in his size, so Meinhardt proudly wore a modified Boy Scout uniform.

Even more... his gift as a speaker made Meinhardt the perfect ground instructor. He taught meteorology and navigation to students. Meinhardt was proud to join the effort to protect America. Meinhardt lived to see the movie "The Wizard of Oz" become a classic. With other "Munchkins," he received a star on the Hollywood Walk of fame and was appreciated by fans across the county.

Meinhardt accomplished much... because Meinhardt never gave up!

Final thoughts…

If this were one of our shows, this is the time when I'd come out in front of the stage and say, "So, what have we learned today?" I hope we've learned a lot.

For me, Walt Disney, P. T. Barnum, and Elvin Bale show us that when our dreams disappear, we can get a bigger dream.

Sandra Day O'Connor, José Hernandez, and Colonel Sanders tell us that "no" doesn't always mean the end of our dreams… we just may have to work a little harder.

Thomas Edison, Michael Jordan, and Mickey Rooney show us that the path to success also includes some failures along the way.

George Washington Carver and Chief Anderson show us that when we do succeed, we can find real happiness by sharing our success and our knowledge with others.

You've made it to the end of this book so I know that you have the drive to finish what you set out to do. That's a gift that each of the people in this book had. I'll remind you once again what my father shared with me long ago…

"You can accomplish almost anything you set your mind to… as long as you're willing to work hard and never give up."

Good luck!

Acknowledgements

We have been blessed to meet or work with several of the people in this book. In no particular order…

Carol Channing was generous with her time, stories, voice, and radiant smile.

Mickey Rooney worked with us on seven productions. He was a focused professional who lived in the present and always focused on the job in front of him.

Meinhardt Raabe had so many inspirational stories of his many adventures. Nothing stopped Meinhardt!

Having between-performance meals with Elvin Bale was a dream come true for a kid who watched in awe every time he performed. Elvin was even more charming as he welcomed us to the Cole Brothers Circus.

Geoffrey Holder was a giant of a man with a bigger than life personality. He shared stories of his struggles and triumphs between recording several shows for us.

Meeting many of the Tuskegee Airmen and having one of them, Ezra Hill, Sr., work with us as a narrator was a lesson in how important and powerful forgiveness can be for the forgiver and the forgiven.

Tony Gabriele's journalistic skills and Nancy Kent Swilley's educator skills were invaluable. I'm lucky to have such smart and generous friends!

Mike Bohme, former director of the Virginia Aviation Museum, commissioned and helped us create our "Wright Brother" show.

Harlan Boll, publicist to Carol Channing, shared many great memories.

Diane Kidd, educator at the Smithsonian National Air and Space Museum is always supportive and encouraging.

Alfred D. Lott, one of "Chief" Anderson's flight students helped us learn what a great teacher and mentor he was.

Ken Riedl and the Watertown Historic Society shared a terrific photo of Meinhardt Raabe.

Rainbow Puppeteers include James Cooper; Wesley Huff; Alyssa Jones; and David, Marcy, and Joshua Messick

Puppets created by Laura Baldwin, Jill Harrington and Frank Lakus.

Glossary

Carbonize – a process that heats an object and turns it to carbon

Commentator – someone who discusses sports or other events, often on radio or television

Distributor – someone who supplies products to stores or other locations

Dyslexia – a difficulty in learning to read

Egress – a way to leave a place, an exit

Filament – a thread of wire or plant materials

Franchise – a business that is allowed to use someone else's ideas or methods

Inappropriate – not proper or suitable

Innovator – someone who creates new ideas

Mentor – someone who helps and guides others

Patent / Patented – an exclusive right to an idea or an invention

Producer – a person or company that makes things to sell, often a job title in the movie and theater business

Profitable – Makes money, is useful

Revolutionize – create a big change

Rotation – to switch from one crop to another every other year

Tourette Syndrome – a disorder causing a person to make unwanted movements or sounds

Bibliography

Alexander, Kerri Lee. "Bessie Coleman." "National Women's History Museum" womenshistory.org, Accessed November 6, 2020.

Channing, Carol. Just Lucky I Guess, A Memoir of Sorts. New York: Simon & Schuster, 2002.

Edwards, Linda McMurry. George Washington Carver: The Life of the Great American Agriculturalist. PowerPlus Books, 2004.

Feiler, Bruce. Under the Big Top, A Season with the Circus. New York: Scribner, 1995.

G., Jacky. "Darth Vader's Stuttering Therapy." "Speech Buddies Blog." Speechbuddy.com, Accessed November 6, 2020.

Gabler, Neal. Walt Disney: The Triumph of the American Imagination. New York: Knopf, 2006.

Geoffrey Holder: The Moment I Lost My Speech Stammer. Washington, DC: National Visionary Leadership Project, 2010.

Hill, Ezra, Sr. The Black Red Tail Angels. Chesapeake: Jones Printing, 2007.

Howard, Tim. The Keeper: A Life of Saving Goals and Achieving Them. New York: Harper-Collins Publishers, 2014.

Iwerks, Leslie. The Hand Behind the Mouse: The Ub Iwerks Story. Los Angeles: Walt Disney Pictures, 1999.

Lakab, Peter. Visions of a Flying Machine. Washington, D.C.: Smithsonian Institution Press, 1990.

"Legends Profile: Michael Jordan." NBA.com, Accessed November 6, 2020.

P.T. Barnum: A Captivating Guide to the American Showman Who Founded What Became the Ringling Bros. and Barnum & Bailey Circus. Captivating History, 2018.

Raabe, Meinhardt with Kinske, Daniel. Memories of a Munchkin. New York: Back Stage Books, 2005.

Rooney, Mickey. Life Is Too Short. New York: Random House, Inc., 1991.

Shadel, Molly Bishop. Litigation and Legal Practice. Chantilly: The Teaching Company, LLC, 2017.

Thomas Edison, The One Who Changed the World. The History Hour, 2019.

Vazquez, Susana. "From Farmer to Astronaut: José Hernandez's Inspiring Story." "The Californian." 2016. thecalifornian.com, Accessed November 6, 2020.

Whitworth, William. "Kentucky Fried." "The New Yorker," 1970. newyorker.com, Accessed November 6, 2020.

Additional quotes from forbes.com. Accessed November 6, 2020 and thefamouspeople.com. Accessed November 13, 2020.

Use of the following names and images is for editorial purposes only and does not imply endorsement by or for the related companies.

"ACADEMY AWARD®" is a trademark and service mark of the Academy of Motion Picture Arts and Sciences

Darth Vader, Luke Skywalker, "Star Wars," and related images are registered trademarks of Lucasfilm, Ltd.

Disneyland, Mickey Mouse, Oswald the Lucky Rabbit, Walt Disney World and related images are registered trademarks of Disney Enterprises.

"Emmy ®" Award is a trademark of the Academy of Television Arts & Sciences and the National Academy of Television Arts & Sciences

Golden Globe is a registered trademark of the Hollywood Foreign Press Association.

Harry Potter and related images are registered trademarks of J.K. Rowling and Warner Brothers Entertainment, Inc.

Kentucky Fried Chicken is a registered trademark of Kentucky Fried Chicken Corporation.

"KFC," and Colonel Sanders images are registered trademarks of KFC Corporation.

Oscar Mayer, Wienermobile and related images are registered trademarks of Kraft Foods Global Brands, LLC

Ringling Brothers and Barnum & Bailey Circus, "The Greatest Show on Earth" are registered trademarks of Ringling Bros.-Barnum & Bailey Combined Shows, Inc.

"Tony Award®" is a trademark of American Theatre Wing, Inc.

Walt Disney and Mickey Mouse Club are registered trademarks of Walt Disney Productions.

David Messick is the founder of Rainbow Puppet Productions. He has written several children's books and dozens of original children's musicals that have been performed at the Smithsonian, New York's American Museum of Natural History, and many other organizations. He has also worked on development projects for the Oprah Winfrey Show and the Disney Channel and worked with many legendary performers. He and his wife Marcy are the parents of two amazing young men… Joshua and Luke. http://davidmessick.com

Liu Light is an illustrator and multimedia designer in New York City. Light has illustrated a number of children's books with a focus on books featuring diverse voices and stories for such organizations as Shout Mouse Press and Rainbow Puppet Productions. They also enjoy drawing animations and comics. http://liulight.com

Other books from David and Liu:

The Amazing Adventures of Chessie the Manatee

Creatures Great and Small

Mary Peake and the Mighty Acorn

Open a Book

The Tall, the Tough, and the Tiny